HEAD OF A GORGON

RAEGEN M. PIETRUCHA

Cover art by Jackie Liu

TABLE OF CONTENTS

For all who have looked in the mirror and seen the snakes.

And to JKK, the best man I've ever known; endless thanks for awaiting me on the other side.

In loving memory of HBP, RCS, and JOP.

Trigger warnings: sexual violence, suicidal ideation

Head of a Gorgon is a narrative in poems that reimagines the myth of Medusa, transporting this tale of sexual violence into contemporary times via persona poems that enable readers to hear this story primarily and directly from a protagonist often sidelined or silenced in other tellings, thereby bringing the visceral physical and psychological experiences and effects of sexual trauma out of the shadows and into the spotlight.

Due to the nature of the subject matter, this book is not recommended for audiences younger than 18 or for survivors of sexual violence who are currently experiencing severe mental and/or physical health issues related to their experiences. A list of resources appears in the back of this book for any reader who may be triggered by its content or may know someone in need of this type of assistance.

FLASH FORWARD

The Gorgon's Parting Thoughts

Silver slash of light like heaven
carve the exit that I've dreamt of
etch until my neck
                    blurts red

past your silver light to soar
me but I only drop instead
like lead thoughts thunk did I not
spit the right red prayers to lift
me up my mouth forgets now
drops words this body can't read
can't breathe or care where thinking
is thunk and hair hisses fix
me but open neck rejects
my head and heads for which home
is unknown because only
not being is free dumb no
more I see no silver but
hear these words thunk my last thought
was flawed was wandering and
wondering why others who
tried to reach me froze but he
could never have been my stone

ORIGINS

Your Captain Speaking

Who cares what other stories have told you?
The water forged you; now your head's

in a sack—no sign of light.
Is your life a blessing or curse, you ask?

Who retains the right to name?

Red Devil Your Mother's mouths
spit water, dreamed only of devouring

God Your Father before
a wave suffocated her.

A kind of flailing
was involved. You don't

remember. Tell you another story. Red Devil Your

Father dreamed only of commanding
water, maimed the gates

of God Your Mother before
his wings were steeped, spent.

A kind of flailing
was involved. You don't

understand. Tell you another story. One day

you dream of freedom,
crack, click a scaly beak in search

of a medium to breathe. But the water's
already grown bored, broke

and mobilized around you, its gaze clear.
A kind of flailing will be involved. There is no

other story. Best to never

be, but here you are,
and the swells are hissing.

This water was never hesitating, just building
and building—then, unzipping, snickering

at you, the prey it ached to drown in its dark.

Sex Ed

came late—spring of eighth grade—before lunch
and after a classmate had trouble

brewing in her stomach already. They put
the job in the hands of an English teacher, Miss Fithie—

pretty, stupid, lean, in the habit of wearing
tight jeans and propping her bottom

on the edge of her desk, easily seen
by boys who would flock to the front for prime

viewing. Slides of the parts that flowers and cartoon
characters had masked for us flashed

as she matched image to word like some game—

but never said what it meant if you'd already seen

more than what appeared
on the screen, never confessed

that naming things commands
nothing. I sat silent like the dumb

majority, wondering what those
kids might be thinking—

interrupted by a hiss of memory
unzipping, something terrible swelling

in me when I thought of these bodies,
another's I was forced to know with my own, and early.

A Snake's Tale

can you keep this secret
    it wouldn't be the first time
        remember
    repeat *I'll keep our secret again*
now hide under here with me
    it's like night
        with the sodium lights
    you look like the orange fish
in my tank
    we're swimming sticky
        with water like the sea
    want to know a secret
I can smell you, fish
    I will show you how to
        be like big girls
    bob your mouth
like a fish now kiss
    kiss me again
        like before
    remember
remember the snake
    in the grass
        won't bite

Collector

I don't remember the first thing
I ever kept. But I would've hidden
it in my pink jewelry box, most
cluttered corner of the closet,

with a dead monarch
butterfly encased in cellophane
and an intact sand dollar, doves
safely inside. It was a good spot

until Mom found a pair
of my stained underwear there.

After that, my hiding places
got smarter. The space under
drawers between rails proved
great for new terms I was tracking

on paper; I scribbled his name
on a notebook cover, then taped
magazine clippings over it,
decorated like other girls did.

The underwear I'd scrub in a creek
in the woods behind our neighborhood.

The best place for anything to hide,
of course, is in plain sight.
I put the shiny rock he gave me,
a gift for keeping his secret,

on top of the dresser by my bed.
Mom and Dad haven't asked where
it came from. It is glittery, gray, harder
than I thought. It wouldn't break

when I threw it at the sidewalk.

The Spring Before Leaving Father

was winter cold and wet
and my damp hair froze at its tips
as I stood at the bus stop

Father marched from the house
across our singed brown yard
hat in hand   yanked it down
around my head

didn't you forget this

*

summer, I'd lure young damselflies
into sleeping jars trimmed with drunk cotton

their tails bouncing   sticking together
blue and green   teasing
neon until the next morning
when I'd run to catch more

the dragonflies I avoided
one tied knots in my hair
spit out hum sounds
'til it settled   dead
in a warm   tangled nest
Father had to cut from my head

*

when I scaled our yard's maple
Father shouted from the open door
that's for dirty boys

and if I didn't come down
he'd strike my shins with a switch

once inside
he'd scrub my hands raw
tell me leaves changed color
because *water means to empty these veins*

because they were dying
which was why I had to abandon them

remember this lesson

*

just before the sun came
and the dirt could thaw   recall how to reclaim

snow turned the world to a skeleton

months in the house
with suspicion stuck in my head
betraying me   creaking
like the floor beneath me   leading
toward a cracked door

another forbidden   frozen surface

Father's face
staring   staring
into his emptied glass

Pray

hail Mother   fueled to erase
my words are with thee
secret arts now uncovered
wickedness muted by thy tune   ceaseless

rotten daughter   your false confession
drops now with this page
the time has come   thy will be done
cleave hurts with opposing motion
give me this way your illuminating dread
and deliver bits of sin into water
as we shiver in nightgowns through this baptism
I'll cede each, pray for their transfiguration
into an illegible whirlpool

Holy Mother   loather of the flawed
I'll retain your blessèd lesson
trust no one now or at any hour
of my remaining breaths

Cheer

The only words I feel safe speaking I scream
alongside a team, combining them
with sharp chops and kicks, a killer

smile. Eleven girls and I devote
our weekdays to memorizing litanies
of victory, and our boys spring higher

each year as if our words
are manna. Atop the pyramid, held
like a house on a rock, my faith

never wavers; I feel the girls' mass
will always lift me as it does the team—
soaring, however briefly,

above enemies—undefeated,
untouchable, immaculate. And on the weekends,
when I can manage to get away from him, I run far

past the fence out back, hide my practice—
a zealot casting spells—hoping the right
words paired with the right actions will someday

help me take some form of flight—
recalling perfectly the patterns and tracts—
vital when you're the only one

who's coming to your defense.

Seeing Stars

*

As a child   I learned this trick

pressed fingertips   to closed eyelids

                made the stars appear

When I opened my eyes

        blurred

           darkness

      Who's there

I couldn't speak what I feared most   believed speaking made *real*

      summoned things into being again

First-grade amnesiac

      late-night TV's snowy stars sizzling

            hoping light

    would scare anything waiting

       in darkness
          to prey

*

Yearning to learn the right kind of kiss

        a blazing in my chest

                a whole universe I could spin

                    hold in like my breath

    until my dizzy head   lovedrunk

                    could overwrite the past

                        hissing in my skull

*

No wonder no boy will love you

Look at you

You don't listen   she said

Then Mother's knuckly yanks raked the lengths of my hair

fingers treading neck   nails puncturing flesh

But no matter how bright

stars are always quiet

couldn't save me

from falling

numb

reminded me to cloak my words

left me

dumb

*

There's nothing extraordinary

        about housing stars

    silenced tragedies adorning

           the engulfing night

To think people strive

      to learn their names

           care about naming them

always waiting for their stupid   distant light to reach

             as if that touch is kind

      Just speaking of them sets them in their searing motion

and from there   no escape

      from their twisted   elliptical fates

Listen

    I'm carving a new star

        in this darkening skin

    I create it

        as easily as I say the words

*

I search for some hero

    some Orion without a loosed belt

        who will sing the lullaby

            that can put me to sleep

        who can sing the song

            that brings me back to dream

But can he exist

        without all those rivets of stars

       Who's there

          still waiting

             for the night

               to rise

PREVALENT STORYLINE

Your Captain Speaking

The men of nets
have their ways. Wives
and daughters play their part, weave

so husbands and sons can leave
at dawn, sweep salted waters with lengths
of trains that callus their hands.

Poverty is obvious. It's the crisp of skin
peeling off the sunburned leather
of a sea-weathered neck. The stink of fish too deep

beneath the nails to be breached. The way
captives will always be clubbed in their traps
as if all smaller creatures were made simply

to pay a penance—the flimsy body buckling,
conferring blood, delivering one last
flail after the strike that finally breaks it

arrives. There is hunger—too much hunger.
Who knows where it comes from.
The day you meet him, your insides grind against

themselves; he lumbers under a palpable
weight of fish from that water—
wet, iridescent prizes glistening.

You pray they'll crush you.
They will. The moment your teeth gnash
meat, you christen him your lord.

M & P's Exchange

I. M's Hunger

What you remind me: I've heard these stories
before—men who part waves, multiply fish.

A flood of thoughts hiss, dissonant, as if
my head brims with the water where we met.

Have you wondered whom you could be with me?
Admittedly, I have imagined two

futures bound, though the space for my pair's face
sat blank as a page. But now that we've met,

my mind veneers yours to hopes so hopeless,
I've rarely ever dared to humor them.

Is it possible a person can heal
a leper through just a single touch, can

prevent the sea's crests from overwhelming,
can feed this famine from a single fry?

II. P's Thirst

The question is, how close will you permit
me to approach? You're a cage for yourself,

and you'd stay there if I let you. I've known
birds like you before, tried my serenades

to charm you out of that place and into
my arms. You claim that you're gripped by the thought

of some version of love, yet you've forged space
so far from me, I fear my hands can't reach

past these rungs to touch you or even toss
you more than a crumb. And how can I save

you from any swell when I'm locked outside
your gate? It's lonely here, a desert so

thirsty it can only think of water.
Is it so wrong to long for just a sip?

III. M's Dilemma

What the sea reminds me:
Desires are like sand—
crude intruders in a day's flow
that stack and stack

until their weight suffocates.
I don't know what to do
with my past besides steep
it silently, slide your hands

away from my skin
when we come in
from the swim.
I've wished I could take

your mind off the water,
its tongues tracing all
the places you wish to be.
I've filled your ears

with my best tunes, but you
continue circling my body,
its salt and scents. I know
what you imagine

with me, but the thought
burns me raw—grains abrading
the luster of the image
of you I worship.

Can there be
no such thing
as love between
us without *that*?

IV: P's Appeal

The way your skin shimmers like the sea
                now it's you who cages me
and this parched pilgrim
                seeks more than just mirage
wants most those keys
                you keep from me
if only you'd concede
                sky without sea is incomplete
if only you were willing to unlatch
                bound with me beyond boundaries
this is what it means
                to be *we*
this is the way
                lovers should be

V: M's Lesson at the Ranch

What desert reminds me:
Secrets can hide from outsiders,
but not from my body—

its curves consumed by sand,
heels up to thighs, back,
and clinging sweaty to my neck.

What if I say more:
Cows don't know
they're fed fat

for slaughter.
Their calves
will forget them.

This knowledge won't change
the patchwork of hide
and land that cloaks daily affairs

like the quilt you lie
over not under us, gnats
swimming in our humidity.

What desert reminds me:
Secrets can hide from outsiders.
But for how long? The hurts my mouth

blurts betray but don't end your quest;
the sand is shadowing, turning a bolder
version of itself; you're bolstered over

me, stained by sweat, sun, dusty stalks
of electrified straw. The sun falls and all
I can do is try to find something sharper

than the pain. Clouds above unravel
sky like hides ripped, revealing the red
of an animal I can't name.

After, I sit in a tub
with no water.
Then I sit on a porch.

It's morning once more.
A herd speaks from the distance.
Too far to see.

The land remembers its lot and feeds it.
The earth remembers its purpose, continues
to break beneath teeth.

VI: P's Recoil

Best forget
        what's happened
                forget about me
        your hands can't trap
this unbridled tide
        unleashed inside
                anything between us
        has passed
like water flees fingers
        like a word spoken
                erases from space
        to make way for others
find another
        to be your waste

Transfiguration

I. Duplicitous Blood

Once, my blood moved nothing like red; then,
ache cut down to the veins, overthrew

the blue liquid my body breathes through;
now that fickle drip sticks

beneath my skin in purpled pools, confused, seeking
a new refuge, as if water or wine could take its place,

as if the sun could stretch far enough to touch and warm me,
as if red could travel far enough back

to resurrect a girl
felled in the grass at sunset.

II. Defeated Wings

My back strains beneath
the weight of a black, broke divinity. Holy leaves flap
in the breeze, but their words don't restore me.

I can't flee this body.
My mind can't find a peak to soar to; the weight
of memory tethers me.

III. Unblinking Eyes

I'd saved my gaze
to search for a hero,
only to find another
predator's conceit.

Now salt singes my sockets.
Vigilant beacons forget
the comfort of closing, refuse
any respite from their watch.

IV. Hardened Hands

Foolish digits will forget
how they almost submitted, cringe
at the thought that they once sought
another's. Battle-bruised knuckles
proved useless, shriek as they bend.

A new mold must be poured.
I swim my hands in.
To burn in gilt now
might make me invincible
once the heat's depleted.

V. Forking Tongue

They might say, with this spoiled mouth, I slander. But they split
me. My tongue senses the stench they left in stereo.

Trespassers treading the end of this plank,
you're the venom I retch from.

VI. Snaking Mane

No body could bear such warfare.

My head delivers riddles

of persistent hisses

forbidden liberation for so long—

twisted hair springs, slithers,

claims my scalp's terrain

and crowns my fate—

thanks to these men,

the oblivious birth of my serpents.

SMASH CUT

Your Captain Speaking

Before the warped doors,
tsunamic squeeze, the gasp
that kick-starts novice parts, before

>your life—

>>do you know—

before blue eyes turn a new
hue, attempt perception
of debt, all seems equal

but is not, was not,
never will be—before
that rule in the form

of hands stamps you with its sour
damp, grope-grope-groping
what you hardly know yourself—

>your self—

>>but who were you—
>>do you know—

your body an odd set
of appended red lessons,
cut gums and the metal-

laced taste of drowning
on your tongue—
before a single sound

abandons your throat,
the catechism has already
begun, your masters' gulls

peck-peck-pecking at your
head, poaching the truth before
you can digest—

you're possessed—

    didn't you know—

before curiosity prickles
and you're lured by a new set
of quick lips and rough digits

to rack you, repeat
the sick rhythm all
victims know by heart—

owe-owe, owe-owe—and it echoes
in the hollowed skull you retrieve
and cleave to, skulk

around with like a Hamlet,
pearl poached
before you could notice

anything more than this story, the undulant
weight your face suffocates under
before you might've realized, but now it's

    too late—

      don't you know—
      to know who you were
      before the terrible happened

Relics

The first to set his sights on me after tried hymns,
but the dissonance struck too similar—

his chords, always choked.

The next pledged devotion,
but another's portrait dropped from his pocket—

his fingers, perpetually outstretched.

Then one came who tried to hide beneath my pane,
but he didn't see the glass was already cracked—

his fractures, natural.

But it's been so long, and there have been so many,
it's hard now to recall how it first felt

to witness the twist seize skin

like ivy, realizing I was the root.
For a while, I'll admit I could live

with hunting understudies;

that seemed the best I could do,
marked for this dark art, my nemeses

too clever, avoiding this perimeter.

I'd settle for some substitute
for justice, torment other gluttons

ignoring the warnings.

I once wished a tender
face could exist with me. But now

I know better. Men keep advancing;

the same gaze awaits; everything
petrifies. This is no life.

No one wishes for kisses that shock white.

Note From the Nadir

No savior awaits. These men are predators,
and every girl, doomed to be consumed by their smoke and mirrors.
I'm testing the edges of shards with my hand,

guessing the distance between cold silver, steaming red.
My life's been a feast of smoke and mirrors.
Best to slice through that meat with my own hand,

put some distance between real and pretend
now that I know the hero I sought will never reach me, doesn't exist.
Can I cut through illusion with my own two hands

as swiftly and easily as my head sopped up what was fed?
I'm certain the dream I chased never existed;
there is no great epiphany.

Yet my head still ingested what was fed.
What can you do when part of the problem is you?
You'd think there'd be some epiphany,

that the equation could be worked out in one's head,
but there's nothing you can do when the problem is you.
Can you solve the problem of your head?

Can you solve that problem with your head?
Try to solve any problem in your head
when the root of the problem is you.

No savior awaits. These men are all the same.
That problem lives in and beyond my brain.
So thank goodness for sharp shards, steadfast hands.

UNCHARTED ENDS

Reinvention Sequence

I. Institutions

If there'd been a Heaven,
it would've known my name
without a label round my wrist.

There'd be more than a glass of water,
bed white as a wedding. My wish missed.
My eyes have reopened in a different room

of the same Hades I always knew. How silly,
to believe there could be any other version
of eternity. The truth is clear as this water

taunting me, trapping that ghastly face I failed
to erase in its glass, framing my mangled nape—
now just another mouth stapled shut.

In what can the silenced place any faith?

A new voice must first be heard to be cure.

II. Hematologic

If I follow this vein,
my neck will remind me,
some words are not so easily bled.

Resurrected, my head surges
again, serpents curling
through my red electric,
burning my circuits hot.

I was loved not. But isn't the scar
worse than the raze that blazed it?

I envy the beasts that make their way
onto my plate; they bleed just once,
and the blow ends their story.

But a life as more than meat may render
a chance for you to sever a tether.

III. Dialyze

All I hold are broken clues,
bruises and blood to patch instead
of glue. The book has implied *Forgiveness
divine*, as if that act can mend, render anything
re-intact, but forgiving these snakes would divide

me in two. Into further forfeit. For my memory runs
thick and deep as blood; its heat can't be
so easily snuffed. *Forgive*, that book
would command. But see my
lack. Of sheer capacity
for. Giving that.

Strip this fiction of its grip by lifting
your eyes from the page to the sky while you
seek the gift no one can take or take back.

IV. Vantage Point

When my eyes try
to gaze high, they espy only
the snakes that have named me.
I've nearly forgotten the blue
that trains the waves in color

beyond this cage
and bolted gate.
When I unfold my wings,
they strain to lift
this serpentine weight.

But you cannot access a new view perched
in the same place forever. To wander
beyond this confine, you must fortify
all facets of you with the skill to fly.

V. Flight Manifest

I once dared to imagine a light
bright enough to illuminate the space
between me and freedom. From my isle,
I thought I saw a route across, thought each word

of this wish could be a dash of a path
marking the way from this sand to new land,
each letter a feather that together could lift
me above and beyond even the vastest abyss.

But isn't this figment?

What if you ditched the blinders, sought your light?
Why choose to keep dwelling in the darkness
of the snakes' den, permit them to constrict
you? Set new sights; look again in your glass,
shimmering like a shield. Haven't we met?

VI. Refraction

My face seems to blur,
warped in this space. Am I
above or beneath this water
oscillating? Did my vision

tunnel too long
through the dark dirt
of the serpents' burrow, drain
from the constant, singular gaze?

As eyes see differently by day than night,
you too can dilate to view beyond sight,
glimpse within and outside. Connect the right
plots. Aim to see more than scales and fangs.
Another face awaits—one you have had
a hand in crafting, choosing now to seek.

VII. Acuity

What's divided me
from me? I search but can't find
the latch to this mask, can't spot

the seams where the snakes bit and split me.

I see I've barely
belonged to me. But what's
a bound, broken bird left to be?

Think a girl lives who hasn't been damaged?
Anything can fracture a fragile wing;
a grounded bird still attempts a flutter.
Why not strive to mend and alight, enter
heavens of your own creating? A new
kind of flight might unwind the serpents' clasp,
transform you from a captive to captain.

VIII. Steeled

My fists wish to curl against
the world of these serpents, but I can't grasp
their slick scales when I drag my brasses.

What good are these hands
if they can't rip villains
from my recesses?

If you sift with them instead, you can search
the debris, separate gems from sand. Hands
can break but do better when creating—
taking that old gray stone instead, turning
it to lead and neutralizing old guiles
through acts these crafters have sharply chosen.
The only way to escape their story:
pen your own, reclaim your territory.

Shedding Skin

~~can~~ you ~~keep this secret~~
    ~~it~~ wouldn't ~~be the first time~~
       ~~remember~~
    ~~repeat *I'll keep our secret again*~~
~~now~~ hide ~~under here with me~~
    ~~it's like night~~
       ~~with the sodium lights~~
    ~~you look~~ like the ~~orange~~ fish
~~in my tank~~
    ~~we're swimming sticky~~
       ~~with water like the sea~~
    ~~want to~~ know ~~a secret~~
~~I can smell you fish~~
    ~~I will show you how to~~
       ~~be like big girls~~
    ~~bob~~ your ~~mouth~~
~~like a fish now kiss~~
    ~~kiss me again~~
       ~~like before~~
    ~~remember~~
~~remember the snake~~
    ~~in the grass~~
       ~~won't~~ bite

IX. Smithing

I don't know where beginnings begin.
I don't know if I can birth one.
I don't know who can be fashioned from fragments.
I don't know what to call such a woman.
I don't know how she'll be fortified.

But are you willing to play such a role?
Are you willing to try to rectify?
Are you willing to forge an unknown whole?
Like faith, let's commit to this blind striving.
Like lightning, let's strike our terms in flashes.
Like fire, let's melt to bridge the divide.
Like a phoenix, we'll cast off the ashes.
From a core eager to molt the old dust,
we'll shape a new woman because we must.

Shedding Skin

The ~~question is, how close will you permit~~
~~me to approach? You're a~~ cage ~~for yourself,~~

~~and you'd stay there if I let you. I've known~~
~~birds like you before, tried my serenades~~

~~to charm you out of that place and into~~
~~my arms. You claim that you're gripped by the thought~~

~~of some version of love, yet you've~~ forged ~~space~~
~~so far from me, I~~ fear ~~my hands can't~~ reach

past these rungs ~~to touch you or even toss~~
~~you more than a crumb? And how can I~~ save

you ~~from any swell when I'm locked outside~~
~~your gate? It's lonely here, a desert so~~

~~thirsty it can only think of water.~~
~~Is it so wrong to long for just a sip?~~

X. Tongue-Tied

My tongue may flail, straining to split
the shackles of these incessant hisses.

So I will start with this nib.
Instead, I will deploy this writ.

A wave may redouble before it breaks,
its sound deafening—but then it dissolves.
And every snake must brumate once the sky
settles into its winter grays. Once gulped
in their smothering gullets, now these words
appear and stick to the page. Not all those
who'd sound use their mouths to speak. Here words stretch
beyond body, soaring with their own wings.
Sound can stream both from fingers and from beaks.
One doesn't always need to speak to sing.

Shedding Skin

~~The way your skin shimmers like the sea~~
       now it's you who ~~cages me~~
~~and this parched pilgrim~~
       seeks ~~more than just mirage~~
~~wants most those keys~~
       ~~you keep from me~~
~~if only you'd concede~~
       ~~sky without sea is incomplete~~
~~if only you were willing to unlatch~~
       ~~bound with me~~ beyond boundaries
~~this is what it means~~
       ~~to be *we*~~
~~this is the way~~
       ~~lovers should be~~

XI. Unfolding

Once upon a time was never mine.
Even before the time I first woke,
that lie has stuck in my throat.

Now I know how the old con goes: A snake
will spin and twist as if these small gestures
could be innocent. But then the scales stretch,
the breadth expands, the corps contorts before
the strike—our parts carved out before our eyes
can even guess which direction we missed.
The deceit is deliberate, leaves us
dazed so other snakes can sink their way in,
flood us with more of that brackish poison.
But I know now too, once you grasp the trick,
then you can begin to dismantle it.

Shedding Skin

~~Best forget~~
    ~~what's happened~~
        ~~forget about me~~
    your hands ~~can't trap~~
~~this unbridled tide~~
    unleashed ~~inside~~
        ~~anything between us~~
    ~~has passed~~
~~like water flees fingers~~
    like a ~~word spoken~~
        ~~erases from~~ space
    to make ~~way for others~~
~~find~~ another
    ~~to be your waste~~

XII. Water Shed

I know what it is to be broken by others, all parts beaten
and lost to another's, as if ocean rules the sand it casts.

And when I realized it had, I wept.
But when I wept, my tears split sea's surface,
and I claimed that throne, became god of salt,
water, shapes, sounds, failing, falling, rising
again. I broke that ocean with a rage
I couldn't contain. Now it undulates
with my tongue, delivers a hymn binding
all other sound to it, even the birds
overhead. Some men thought they'd be able
to rule this water forever, but none
can stop this sound. When my ocean first spoke,
the serpents nested in my head recoiled.

XIII. Loosed

I no longer place any faith in the fables of snakes.

Belief in such claims rendered me a slave.
Only cold blood lives inside of those men;
they raid and feed off the heat of their slaves.
It's true that they did invade this body;
they couldn't retain the mind of this slave.
They'll never touch an ounce of me again,
never again taste the meat of this slave.
I didn't have to part to crack their trap;
skin hinges to stay intact, not enslaved.
Now I see they couldn't really steel me;
I've forged this new gun for a former slave.
My target is truth, and I shoot to save.
I aim for it with the words that I made.

XIV. Ginosko

Dust dances in the sun now, so tiny
the air meets it as sea, and the grains gild
the leaves of my plants. As I water them,
I recall how a woman I once knew
used to keep strings-of-pearls just like the one
I now have. It struck me so suddenly,
finally feeling one of the tendrils;
despite the distance, she and I shared life;
I might just be tending to her garden.
Then, I recognized man's world would persist
with its spinning; I recognized not all
our sisters have been able to seize peace;
I recognized countless questions remain,
with answers I must continue to seek.

DENOUEMENT
(THE WOMAN'S PARTING THOUGHTS)

Questions to P

At first, my only consolation
was, you weren't the first.
How can you steal what's already been stolen?

But weren't you always up for a challenge?
The notes between us spelled no, but
you wouldn't hear it, so my next consolation

was, you only happened once.
I may not have been able to best your worst—
How can you envenom what's already poison?—

but it turns out I could out-turn your terms,
capsize your lies, chart a course no snake could discover.
Then my consolation

evaporated like morning mist from a waterfront.
A new face awaited me there.
How could you have ever found what was unfounded?

Then came this realization:
The joke has always been on you, I fear.
What need is there for consolation
once a girl's found her champion?

Questions to a Snake

Tell me—I can't remember—
where did you first enter,
and tell me, how many other

times had you tracked me before?
When did you first slither
into me, before I could remember,

start bolting my cage, edge my talons sharper?
Did nothing register through the budding feathers,
tiny cries? How many other

times did circumstance order
you to play a role besides hunter?
You see, now I can remember your face elsewhere,

options beyond the unkindness you favored—
hooking fish, downing birds.
But I'm not built like my mother;

I won't keep your evil submerged.
You didn't count on a deviation from the pattern.

So tell me what was never there for me to remember:
Were there others? No—*how many* others?

Mumfish

Mother, why didn't you protect your daughter?
I told you about the beast so long ago
but struggled alone under the weight of his water.

When he invaded my borders,
you pretended it was nothing, muffled his name in a bubble.
Mother, why didn't you protect your daughter?

Did you do it to retain some type of order
for the low, low cost of a good you thought expendable?
I flailed under the weight of his water

as if it were burial—which I suppose is called for
when the smallest snag can make great yarns unravel.
But, Mother, why didn't you protect your daughter?

A parent (and a woman too) could've easily ended the torture,
broken the tides that would follow. The irony here is less than subtle.
I nearly drowned under the weight of his water,

unarmed, unable to swim from the slaughter.
Sometimes I wonder if you would've missed me at all.
Mother, I'll never know why you didn't protect your daughter.

I'm still searching for a way through the weight of that water.

Ravenfather

You didn't make me raven, Father; unkindness did.

You didn't see who split your girl too soon from the shell,
couldn't hear the shivers of downless skin.

You only ever saw me after,
these dark hinged wings.

A double life already begun.
One father, two masters, but sentry? I had none.

*

I was so happy you sat with me, Father,
in the hospital.

Diagnosis: Half-raven with two brains reigning my head;
flapping, falling back through memory, finding only endless twisted slacks.

Half-raven with black breast cracked open,
blue tumor beating back-forth, forth-back behind viperous ribs.

Unkindness, it seems, runs in this blood.
Halves foreign to each other struggle to fit, incurably different.

*

You asked me what I saw in my reflection once, Father,
not knowing the tenor of your question.

When I'd perch before a surface,
I'd mostly notice shadows, what's stuck with things beneath a shined light.

You said, *You can tell me anything.*

I'd waited two lifetimes for any man's kindness to reach me.

And I returned it,
tucked words no bird should ever know under tongue.

*

Fledglings can't be heroes, Father;
the small don't dare spring with unversed wings.

They recite terms they've heard but can't grasp,
rattles demanding salvation: Deliver us from—

How swiftly a flock of unkindness will wisen us.

Then we pray for age or an end, invent reticent melodies,
peck and peck at our binding ties.

*

You'd be so proud now—this sharp beak of mine.

Split for collision, my halves now collaborate,
fray unkindness' grip like scissors.

Father, sometimes I saw your black pain flapping.
But birds can never remain in sky.

Why should I name who happened?
Could that ever measure their infinite unkindness?

Let me share these notes instead.

Forgive what I've hidden in this odd soldered shell;
trust the blind flight alongside shadows I must shepherd.

Your daughter's a crux, but recovered from the squall, resolved,
shaping a haven with these pitchy songs.

NOTES

"Your Captain Speaking" (1) is for LS.

"Sex Ed" is for KT.

"Note From the Nadir" is for LM.

"XIV: Ginosko" (part of "Reinvention Sequence") is for HBP.

"Ravenfather" is for KRP.

GRATITUDE

Thank you, Freddy La Force, for believing in this work and sharing it with the world through Vegetarian Alcoholic Press. M's is not an easy story, but you embraced her and it fiercely, and I will always be grateful for it.

Larissa Szporluk — advisor, mentor, teacher, friend — I am graciously indebted to you. I didn't know this was the book I would write, but I do know this was the book I needed to write, and I also know you saw this well before I did. Thank you for the breadcrumbs you dropped early in the process that lit the way along my journey.

Many thanks to Wendell Mayo, who crossed genres to take me under his wing and provided insights on the narrative structure beneath the poetic musings of our M. I wish you were here to hold this in your hands and read these words. You are sorely missed.

Gratitude to several teachers I had along the way whose encouragement and care led me to the door of my creative writing journey: Miss Buckman, Miss Loss, Ann Guido, Pamela Gautier, and Joseph Jones; and those professors who guided me past it: Luci Tapahonso, Diza Sauers, Dorothy Barresi, Leilani Hall, and the late Lary Gibson. Thanks as well to my fellow workshoppers along the way, especially those who witnessed M come to life and enriched her story through their drawings, dialogue, and more. Special thanks to Brad Aaron Modlin and Abigail Cloud in particular for taking the time to sit with this version and so generously share thoughts on it for the cover.

Speaking of the cover, thank you, Jackie Liu, for taking the concept I had so amateurishly sketched to try to match my verbal version and vision of M, then creating such a powerful piece of art that I can't even imagine this book existing at all without your stunning contribution to it.

Thanks to my family for continued lessons in the unconditional. Thanks to E, KZ, KC, and GC, who saw me through the darkest days and led me into the light. Thanks to JKK, for finding and recognizing me there. And thanks to the light, which was always waiting, and which outlasted the darkness.

ACKNOWLEDGEMENTS

Many thanks to the following journals for believing in my work and first publishing the following poems, some as variations of and/or with different titles of the versions herein:

Cimarron Review — "The Spring Before Leaving Father"

Clackamas Literary Review — "Seeing Stars"

Euphony — "Cheer"

Feral: A Journal of Poetry and Art — "Relics"

Four Chambers — "Sex Ed"

Juke Joint — "M & P's Exchange" and "Note From the Nadir"

Naugatuck River Review — "Collector"

Paper Nautilus — "Your Captain Speaking" (2)

Persephone's Daughters — "Transfiguration"

Punk Noir Magazine — "Reinvention Sequence"

Sakura Review — "Your Captain Speaking" (1)

Vita Brevis — "The Gorgon's Parting Thoughts"

Wine Cellar Press — "Questions to a Snake"

Additionally, I'd like to express my gratitude to *Puerto del Sol* and *Edge* for publishing early versions of individual sections of the lengthier "Reinvention Sequence" and "M & P's Exchange" poems, respectively, and to *Fevers of the Mind* for reprinting a five-poem feature excerpted from this collection.

I am also grateful to Two of Cups Press for selecting my chapbook, *An Animal I Can't Name*, as the winner of its 2015 chapbook contest and publishing several of the poems included in this manuscript, including "Pray," "Your Captain Speaking" (3), "Mumfish," and "Ravenfather" for the first time.

PLAYLIST

When creating a playlist for *Head of a Gorgon*, I decided to take a persona approach to it as well, having each poem look into a sort of musical mirror. What song echoed or spoke to what I was exploring in each particular poem? What song would be each poem's doppelganger?

By the end of this exercise, I ended up with a rather epic playlist of 37 songs, which I distilled down to the following 20 songs. The ever-generous Meggie Royer published my annotated list with the rationale behind several song selections on *Persephone's Daughters'* website; the music-only version can be found on YouTube via the Head of a Gorgon channel. Links to both versions can also be found on my website at raegenmp.wordpress.com.

"The Mission" by Puscifer (mirror of "Your Captain Speaking" (1))
"Beautiful Secrets" by Sarah Blasko (mirror of "Sex Ed")
"Sullen Girl" by Fiona Apple (mirror of "Collector")
"21" by Cranberries (mirror of "Pray")
"Cough Syrup" by Young the Giant (mirror of "Cheer")
"Running Up That Hill" by Kate Bush (mirror of "M & P's Exchange, I: M's Hunger")
"Strange & Beautiful" by Aqualung (mirror of "M & P's Exchange, IV: P's Appeal")
"Carnival" by Tori Amos (mirror of "M & P's Exchange, V: M's Lesson at the Ranch")
"Water Baby" by Sneaker Pimps (mirror of "M & P's Exchange, VI: P's Recoil")
"Fell on Black Days" by Soundgarden (mirror of "Transfiguration")
"This Place Is a Prison" by The Postal Service (mirror of "Your Captain Speaking" (3))
"Light Switch" by Jaime Wyatt (mirror of "Relics")
"Mad World" by Gary Jules (mirror of "Note From the Nadir")
"Dead Things" by Emiliana Torrini (mirror of "Reinvention Sequence, I: Institutions")
"Roads" by Portishead (mirror of "Reinvention Sequence, VI: Refraction")
"Sweet Talk" by The Killers (mirror of "Reinvention Sequence, VII: Acuity")
"Sing" by Dresden Dolls (mirror of "Reinvention Sequence, X: Tongue-Tied")
"Apres Moi" by Regina Spektor (mirror of "Reinvention Sequence, XII: Water Shed")
"Control" by Poe (mirror of "Questions to a Snake")
"Hide and Seek" by Imogen Heap (mirror of "Mumfish")

RESOURCES

The following is a nonexhaustive list of organizations that support survivors of sexual violence:

In the U.S.

RAINN (Rape, Abuse & Incest National Network):
National Sexual Assault 24/7 Hotline: 1-800-656-HOPE (4673)
Online chat: online.rainn.org
Email through webform at rainn.org/contact-us

National Sexual Violence Resource Center (NSVRC):
Hotline: 877-739-3895
Email through webform at nsvrc.org/contact

International

Rape Crisis Network Europe
Links to direct websites supporting survivors worldwide (not only in Europe) can be found at rcne.com/links/sources-of-help-for-survivors/.

Additional international rape crisis hotlines can be found through ibiblio.org/rcip/internl.html.

ABOUT THE AUTHOR

Raegen M. Pietrucha writes, edits, and consults creatively and professionally. *Head of a Gorgon* is her debut poetry collection. Her poetry chapbook, *An Animal I Can't Name*, won the 2015 Two of Cups Press competition, and she has a memoir in progress. She received her MFA from Bowling Green State University, where she was an assistant editor for *Mid-American Review*. Her work has been published in *Cimarron Review*, *Puerto del Sol*, and other journals. Connect with her at raegenmp.wordpress.com.